FLOWERS
OF A
WOODLAND SPRING

FLOWERS
OF A
WOODLAND SPRING

CAROL LERNER

William Morrow and Company
New York 1979

Printed in the United States of America.   First Edition   1 2 3 4 5 6 7 8 9 10

Library of Congress Cataloging in Publication Data

Lerner, Carol.
Flowers of a woodland spring.

Summary: Describes the woodland wild flowers known as ephemerals
  and presents some specific examples.
1. Wild flowers—Juvenile literature. [1. Wild flowers] I. Title.
QK85.5. L47   582'.13'09152   78-32154
ISBN 0-688-22190-4
ISBN 0-688-32190-9 (lib. bdg.)

By the Same Author
On the Forest Edge

FOR
NANCY
HART

This day in early spring has begun wet and dull. A soft rain chills the morning air and darkens the ashy gray trunks of the beeches and maple trees. Their rain-stained branches seem as bare and cold as trees in winter.

High overhead there are thousands of buds swelling with the year's new growth, but the young leaves have not yet burst from the dark-brown scales that cover them. From the ground the twigs above look dark and lifeless.

Even the birds are still. They huddle in the shelter of last night's perches, finding some protection from the wetness of the morning. Among all the bare branches above, the only sign of life is a fox squirrel's winter nest, a shapeless heap of leaves tucked in the nook of a maple's limbs.

Last year's leaves lie wet and heavy on the ground, soaked by the rain that falls upon them. But the forest floor does not seem to belong in the same season with the bare-branched trees above. Here below, the earth has already been changed by spring.

Every inch of ground seems to have small green leaves poking up from beneath the brown leaf cover. The new leaves come in all kinds of shapes—some long and stringy, others broad and pointed. There are clumps of feathery silver-green leaves and other bright floppy ones that cover whole patches of the earth. On stalks above these leaves, the flowers of the spring woodland are in bloom. They are small, pale, and delicate, and there are so many of them that they have turned the woods into a huge flower bed. The flowering carpet starts on each side of the path and covers all the ground, right into the crannies between the roots of the trees.

Compared to most growing things, these little flower plants have appeared with the suddenness of an explosion. Just a month earlier, the ground showed little color except for the drab brown-leaf litter. Even two weeks ago, the first reddish leaves of the spring beauties and the pointed shoots of trout lily gave only a hint of what was coming.

Now they are in full flower, at the peak of their display. But before another month has gone, many of these plants will seem to disappear again. They will make seeds, their leaves will shrivel up, and they will be gone from sight until next spring. They begin to wither by the time the leaves of the forest trees are fully grown. Once the maples and beeches have leafed out, the trees form a green canopy that shades the ground of the woods. Layers of leaves will block out the sunshine that these plants need to make their food. Even on the brightest day of summer, the forest floor will be dark and damp and cool. So these little flowers are in a race with the forest canopy.

This group of plants is called the woodland spring "ephemerals." The word *ephemeral* means that they appear aboveground for only a very short time. They grow in the deciduous forests all over the eastern half of the United States. Their pattern of life is different from the lives of most of the other woodland plants that grow beside them.

The woodland ephemerals are sun plants, growing in a place that is shady during most of the growing season. They succeed in this habitat because they complete the whole of the aboveground part of their life cycle very quickly.

For these few weeks of the year the ephemerals dominate the woods, although other spring flowers—bloodroots and bellworts and jack-in-the-pulpits—stand in little groups above them. The ephemerals bloom in such great numbers and grow so thickly that their disappearance by the time summer comes is hard to believe.

Of course, they don't really vanish. They continue to live, secretly, under the leaf litter in the top few inches of the earth. This spongy black soil has been made from the rotted leaves of earlier years. Buried here are the thousands of little plant food storehouses that enable the plants to burst from the earth on the first warm days of spring.

Like most other woodland plants, these ephemerals are perennials. Their underground parts stay alive from year to year, even though the stems and leaves above the ground die down. Before the tree canopy has closed and their leaves die, the ephemerals will make food that will be kept in underground organs all through the winter. These storage organs are known

as rhizomes, tubers, corms, or bulbs, depending upon the details of their structure.

Even though they grow down in the earth, these plant parts do not belong to the root system of the plants. They are all underground stems, but they have different forms from stems that grow aboveground and support the leaves and flowers.

Rhizomes are underground stems that usually grow level with the earth's surface. As long as the plant remains alive, the rhizome will continue to grow each year. Some are thin and others are rather thick, but they all contain stored food for the plant.

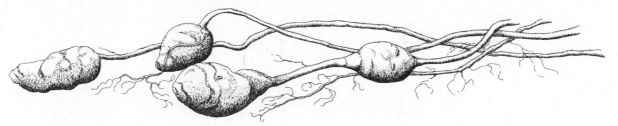

Underground stems of certain other plants become very fat and swollen in some places as they fill with food. These thick parts are tubers.

Corms and bulbs are a little different. The corm is short and thick like a tuber, but it usually grows in an upright position.

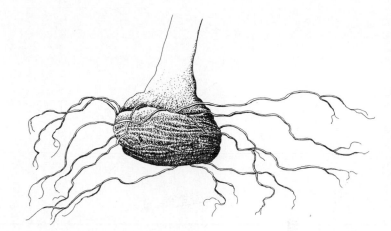

Bulbs also grow upright, but the underground stem in a bulb is only the short part at its bottom. Most of the food in a bulb is not in the stem itself, but in the thick scales that grow up from it. The scales are really a different kind of leaf and make up the largest part of the bulb.

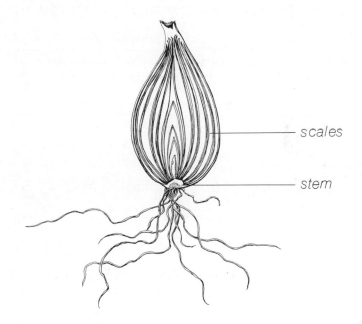

scales

stem

In the ground the plant's food is hidden from animals looking for something to eat and protected from the freezing cold. Then with the first warming days of spring, the plant uses the food to put up leaves and flowers with dramatic speed.

Even before the winter comes, the ephemerals get a headstart on next spring's growth. Using the stored food, the plants send out new roots in the fall and develop underground shoots that will become the aboveground parts of the plants in spring. Even the flower buds of next year, in miniature and protected by scaly coverings, will be formed on the underground parts of the plants before the winter shuts down plant activity.

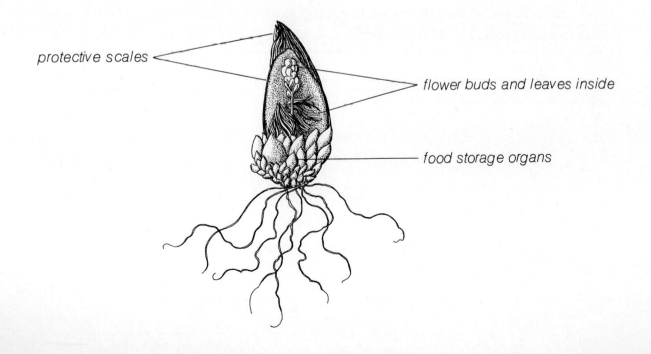

protective scales

flower buds and leaves inside

food storage organs

Most of the other spring-flowering plants have the same kinds of underground storage organs as the ephemerals. They also form underground buds before the winter comes, so they can make the same kind of quick growth in early spring.

But unlike the ephemerals, the leafy parts of these other flowers will live through the months of summer. When only broken sunlight strikes the forest floor in July, the trilliums and Solomon's seals and jack-in-the-pulpits will stand with green leaves and slowly ripening fruit. They are really shade plants, and their leaves will be able to make food even in the shadows of summer.

Among the many kinds of spring wild flowers growing in the forest, only a handful belong to the ephemerals. One of the most common is the spring beauty. Often it covers the ground with mats of leaves and blossoms.

The food supply of the spring beauties is stored in a little corm that usually looks like a flattened pea, though it may be as much as two inches thick. At the top of this corm, the tiny buds are covered by brown scales during the fall and the winter. In earliest spring, stringy leaves and flower stalks push above the leaf litter. Each stalk has a loose cluster of white or pink flowers, with fine pink lines marking the petals.

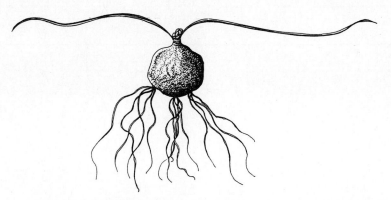

The toothwort is another ephemeral with pale flowers. It also has small blossoms of white or pale pink, and when it grows among the spring beauties, the two plants are hard to tell apart at first. But the toothwort is taller and more upright. Below its cluster of flowers is a whorl of leaves. Each of these leaves is divided into narrow sections with toothed edges.

The plant is nourished by the food that was stored last year in a slender rhizome underground. Because the crisp little rhizome has a sharp peppery taste, the plant is also called "pepper root."

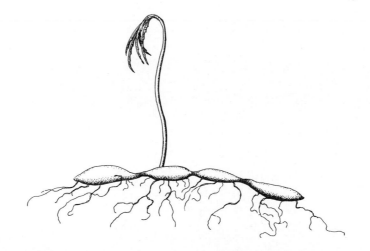

Dutchman's-breeches nod above mounds of soft fernlike leaves. The heap looks silvery when the breeze stirs the leaves and shows their lighter undersides. The flowers, shaped like floppy pants turned upside down, are white with a yellow tip on the bottom. Leaves and flower stalks grow out from clusters of small pink corms just belowground.

A close relative is the squirrel corn. The leafy parts of this plant look the same as the Dutchman's-breeches. Its flowers bloom about a week later and are white or light pink. The plant gets its name from the shape of the storage organs. These parts often grow right at the surface of the ground, and sometimes they can be seen by taking away the litter of dead leaves just under the plant. They look like fat grains of yellow corn scattered carelessly on the earth.

Another woodland ephemeral,
the wild leek, has a different pattern
of growth. It too is one of the
earliest leafy plants of the forest
floor. Large flat leaves of light green
grow from an underground bulb
and then send the food they
make back down to the bulb.
The leaves completely cover the
ground in places where the plant
grows thickly. They have a strong
onion smell and taste.

But then, before the plant
flowers, the leaves start to wither.
After they are gone, early in the
summer, a leafless stalk will grow
from the bulb and a clump of
white flowers blooms at its tip.

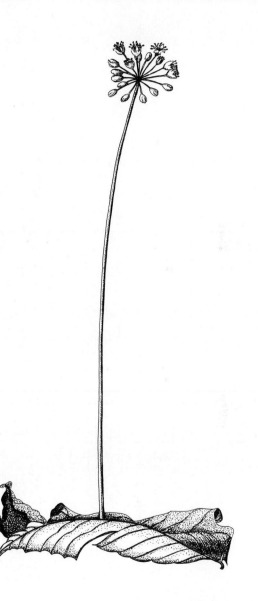

The single yellow flower of the trout lily nods between two pointed leaves that are streaked with darker markings. On sunny days masses of trout lilies make a graceful splash of color on the forest floor. The blossoms close at night and when it is cloudy.

Young plants that grow from seeds have only a single narrow leaf. Four years or more are needed before the plant becomes fully grown, with a pair of leaves and a flower. But the plant that flowers this year makes food for a new bulb that will produce a flowering plant again next year.

With the warmer days of late spring, the sun is higher in the sky. It shines through the leafy green ceiling of the beech and maple trees. Now the great mass of young and growing leaves in the forest is high in the treetops. Down below, the ephemerals have started to wither and are making their quick retreat from the forest floor.

Soon there will be no reminder of their short parade in the sunlight. But before the cold of winter comes, little flowers will form under dull scales. They will lie underground in these wrappings for half a year longer. Then once again the ephemerals will push up through the matted crust of dead leaves to celebrate another woodland spring.